ECK WISDOM
on
Spiritual
Freedom

ECK WISDOM

on

Spiritual Freedom

HAROLD KLEMP

ECKANKAR
Minneapolis
www.Eckankar.org

ECK Wisdom on Spiritual Freedom

Copyright © 2018 ECKANKAR

The terms ECKANKAR, ECK, EK, MAHANTA, SOUL TRAVEL, and VAIRAGI, among others, are trademarks of ECKANKAR, PO Box 2000, Chanhassen, MN 55317-2000 USA.   180510

Printed in USA

Photo of Sri Harold Klemp (page 91)
by Art Galbraith

Library of Congress Cataloging-in-Publication Data

Names: Klemp, Harold, author.

Title: ECK wisdom on spiritual freedom / Harold Klemp.

Description: Minneapolis : Eckankar, 2018.

Identifiers: LCCN 2018041413 | ISBN 9781570434686 (pbk. : alk. paper)

Subjects: LCSH: Eckankar (Organization--Doctrines. | Liberty--Religious aspects--Eckankar (Organization)

Classification: LCC BP605.E3 K55388 2016 | DDC 299/.93--dc23 LC record available at https://lccn.loc.gov/2018041413

CONTENTS

What Is Spiritual Freedom? 1

How Soul Finds Freedom 4

Steps to Spiritual Freedom 7

The Desire for Spiritual Freedom 16

The Key to Liberation. 27

Purpose of the ECK Teachings 34

Secrets of Mastership 37

You Came Here to Fly 42

You Can Go Beyond. 47

Spiritual Exercises: Try Out
   Your Wings 52

Questions and Answers 56

Which Way Now?. 72

WHAT IS SPIRITUAL FREEDOM?

The Blackfoot Indians tell this story:

While climbing in an area of steep cliffs, an Indian brave came upon an eagle's nest. There were several eggs in the nest, and he managed to steal one and carry it back to his village. He placed the egg in a hen's nest, and after it hatched, the young eagle followed the mother chicken about and grew up believing itself to be a chicken. All day the young eagle walked about with its head lowered to the ground in the same way the chickens did, scratching in the dirt, pecking at worms and seeds.

One day, when the eagle was fully

grown, he looked up and saw a magnificent bird soaring in the heavens. He went to the old grandmother hen, who knew many things about the world, and asked, "What's that bird, Grandma?"

"That's an eagle," the old chicken said.

"How wonderful it must be to fly like that," the young eagle said, looking up at the great bird.

"Yes," Grandma said, nodding in agreement, "but you must forget about flight. You are a chicken."

So the eagle spent his life scratching in the dirt with the chickens.

Soul is an eagle, but we must recognize our identity. As an eagle, we have to accept the responsibility of being ourselves and not react to other people's emotions, viewpoints, and efforts to control us.

We have to be cause in our own lives and not the effect of others. That is the difference between being a free man and a slave.

Spiritual freedom is living to your full potential—heart, mind, and Soul. What could be more satisfying?

How Soul Finds Freedom

Spiritual freedom is growing into a state of more godliness. Becoming more aware of the presence of God. How do you do this? By becoming aware of the lessons behind your everyday experiences. This is how you grow into a loving awareness of the presence of God.

Spiritual freedom is a difficult topic to talk about, because in the grand view of things, spiritual freedom means to be free of whatever is causing us problems here.

"Rosa" has had many serious problems that have not crushed her, but which have developed in her a lightness of heart and a sense of humor. One day, at her favorite farm, she lost her car keys. She had meant to fill her car with plump pumpkins, sun-flowers, and other flowers. But now?

Where were those car keys?

This is when her thirty years in Eckankar, and life's experiences, saved the day. She declined to fret, choke back tears, or feel abandoned—some usual reactions. Instead, she joked with the men who worked at the farm.

"Does your little dog know how to find keys?"

"If they smell like chicken, he can find them," one replied.

Rosa laughed, actually laughed, with her keys lost. No crying!

Then her inner guidance showed her a picture of where the keys were. They were in the paper which wrapped a bouquet of fresh-cut flowers just purchased.

So she realized that the usual reactions of panic, anxiety, and fear would have cut off her inner guidance from Spirit. But spiritual detachment and thirty years of ECK training had allowed her to return home with all her planned-for bounty.

Rosa, then, had two things in her favor: a sense of humor and a complete trust in Divine Spirit.

This is how ordinary life events test our wings. Will we accept freedom from our habits of opinion, emotion, reaction? Will we trust the divine goodness of Spirit to lead us to a higher path?

The ultimate state of spiritual freedom brings wisdom, love, and spiritual power. But there are stages in between. We expand or unfold from no freedom into a greater state of spiritual freedom.

STEPS TO SPIRITUAL FREEDOM

A First Step to Freedom Is Self-Responsibility

*W*hat does the path of ECK offer people? It offers self-responsibility.

You say, "Self-responsibility? Gee, thanks. Life's hard enough." But ECK also offers spiritual freedom. I don't know if there's a way to get spiritual freedom unless you first develop self-responsibility.

How do you do that? By putting your attention on God in the right way.

One example is the song of HU.

Going to the Temple within Yourself

When you sing or chant *HU*, an ancient name for God, you are spiritualizing your

7

attention. You are saying, "I am putting all my attention, heart, and soul upon the highest good that I can imagine" instead of saying, "God, I'm having such a hard life; please help me out of this or that."

You are learning how to come into contact with the temple within—the most sacred part of yourself—and the Inner Master. You get your own answers so that you can go through life with self-mastery.

In that sense, you come to the point where you no longer have to ask someone in authority, "Give me my answers. Tell me, am I going to have a successful life?"

When you come to the point of self-mastery, as you are working toward it, you learn that you can shape your own future. You are making your own present through self-responsibility and the attention on the Sound and Light of ECK at the temple within yourself. Sound and Light are simply God's love in action.

Taking Spiritual Action

Returning from a business trip in the Middle East, two ECKists stopped in Greece for a holiday before continuing on to the United States to attend an Eckankar seminar. The two young men passed through customs, unaware that they were supposed to declare the money they were carrying into the country.

Everything went fine until it was time to leave Greece. At the airport they were stopped at customs and searched. The officials discovered they were carrying money, but the two ECKists didn't have a declaration to prove they'd had it when they entered the country. They were taken to a jail cell, a small, narrow room with one dirty mat on the floor, with the threat of having to serve a minimum six-month jail sentence.

The ECKists were permitted to contact the embassy of their country. An embassy representative said he would try to figure out some way to get them released. "But," he added, "it doesn't look very good for you. You could be here a long time."

After the embassy spokesman left, one of the ECKists began to chant *HU*. His companion joined him. Later they read from *The Shariyat-Ki-Sugmad*, the holy scripture of Eckankar, which they had been allowed to take into the cell.

The purpose of the ECK books is to spiritualize the individual's consciousness. This is why it helps to read from one of the books before you do a contemplation. But if you find yourself in trouble, a good way to spiritualize yourself quickly is to simply chant *HU*.

The two ECKists read and chanted throughout the night. In the morning, accompanied by the Greek attorney assigned to defend them, they appeared before the magistrates. Their defense was further complicated by the fact that the attorney was not fluent in their language.

The ECKists explained that they hadn't intended any harm, nor did they realize they were being dishonest by entering the country without declaring their money. But justice in the Greek court system is very definite: In cases such as this, regardless of one's motives, breaking the law means a long jail sentence.

After the arguments were heard, the three magistrates retired to their chambers to deliberate the case. When they came back to the courtroom, they declared the ECKists not guilty. Furthermore, their money would be returned, and they would be allowed to leave the country. The verdict was so unexpected that the entire courtroom burst into applause.

The ECKists had found themselves in a very bad situation, but they found their way out of it simply by remembering to chant

HU and put their attention upon the ECK, the love of God.

A story like this has good value because it illustrates how the power of Divine Spirit works in a real-life situation when you follow the true path of Light and Sound, for ECK is the path of life.

All People Make Their Own World

God has placed each Soul upon earth to gain the spiritual purity and experience It needs to become a Co-worker with God. From the very beginning, many lifetimes ago, Soul made blunders. It was like an infant first having to find out how to crawl, then walk, while learning its place in the family and society.

Growth and development are a natural part of the divine order.

The ECK teachings say that people create karma, a debt with Divine Spirit, by ignorance of divine law. Time and experience will teach them better. However, it usually takes lifetimes to work off karma, because people forget their divine nature. This forgetfulness shows up in anger, vanity, greed, and other harmful traits. The result is more karma.

For that reason, we speak of the wheel of karma and reincarnation. More karma brings on more lifetimes. However fast people run, they must go even faster to stay ahead of their deeds, which threaten to catch and swallow them. Is there no end to this cycle?

There surely is.

After an individual has passed so many lives in one religion or another, been whipped this way and that by life, it eventually dawns on him there is no way to beat the game alone. All running gets him is more running.

At this point, a change occurs, perhaps as spiritual doubt. Or maybe it's a vision. A large percentage of people in the United States claim at least one vision, a strong and unforgettable dream, or an out-of-body experience.

That experience is a wake-up call from the Mahanta, the Living ECK Master, an inner and outer spiritual guide.

From that moment on, they become the seekers.

Yet they may spend the rest of this life in the church of their youth, too scared to leave it for a path like ECK, which gives them more satisfying answers. They are still the seekers. Perhaps in the next lifetime, they will find the courage to say, "What am I doing here? What is the meaning of life?"

Eckankar can show all people the most direct route home to God.

What about spiritual freedom? It is Soul's final release from the Law of Karma and reincarnation.

Love is the force that returns Soul to

God. For the path of truth starts in the heart, and the journey home to God begins with meeting the Mahanta in either a dream or in person. The Spiritual Exercises of ECK give strength and comfort, for these simple daily contemplations give one a stronger bond with the Divine Being. We call the path of ECK the Easy Way.

So the main benefit of ECK is spiritual freedom.

The entire aim of life is to find that freedom. Though the earth may shake and tremble, the person who loves God above all else will endure with peace of heart and mind.

THE DESIRE FOR
SPIRITUAL FREEDOM

"Maria," from Mexico, met the ECK Master Fubbi Quantz seven years before she ever heard of the ECK teachings.

ECK Masters are spiritual beings who help people find true freedom. Throughout the ages, they have given encouragement, aid, and divine love to seekers at every stage of unfoldment.

At the time, Maria was working in a store in Mexico City. It was a good store, and she liked the owners, who sold valuable art, paintings, and old books.

Maria had planned to take off from work for forty-five days to travel to Europe with

16

her husband. But it meant leaving her little girls at home. As she considered this situation, Maria felt a strong reluctance to go on the vacation.

One day, near the departure date, an old man entered the shop. He looked like a native of India, yet he addressed her in perfect English.

Another of the sales clerks said to Maria, "You speak English. Would you like to help him?" So Maria approached the man with a warm and friendly smile.

While they talked, she was struck by his genuine kindness. He was so very kind and courteous. And when he spoke, the words flowing from his mouth were more than casual, ordinary ones, for they were like priceless pearls of wisdom. Each shone with an unmistakable luminescence.

Their conversation lasted for some time. At length he said, "You're always smiling, but why are your eyes so sad?"

She said, "I think maybe it's because I don't have freedom inside myself. I have freedom out here, but I don't have it inside."

He said, "Ah, yes. Spiritual freedom. You want spiritual freedom."

What did he mean by spiritual freedom? As if reading her thoughts, the old man pulled a coin from his pocket and showed it to her. On the coin was a face.

"Look carefully at this silver coin," he said. "See the face on it?" Maria studied the face.

"The person on the face of this coin is trying to lead people to spiritual freedom," the old gentleman continued. "I would like you to have this coin."

"I can't just take your coin," she said.

He persisted. "Please, take it," he said. "It will always remind you of spiritual freedom."

Finally she took it. Soon after, she and

her husband began their trip to Europe. First stop was Spain. They also decided on a quick side trip to Italy, where Maria got a strong sense of déjà vu. Had she ever lived there in a past life? Things were very familiar. Too familiar to be a coincidence.

And in the quiet alcoves of her mind there lingered the matter of the silver coin. What had the old man in the shop meant by spiritual freedom?

Yet not until seven years later did Maria encounter the teachings of ECK. It happened like this:

During a visit to a local ECK Center, she saw drawings of the ECK Masters. One was of the ECK Master Fubbi Quantz. Looking at the drawing, Maria felt an overwhelming wave of love and gratitude sweep over her. Why, that was the very gentleman she'd met in the store!

Maria had found the secret of love. The secret lay in the teachings of ECK, for it was

ECK Master Fubbi Quantz who'd introduced the fountain of divine love into her
life.

Like many so many other people, Maria
had spent her entire life searching for divine
love. And until she'd found the ECK teachings, life was like a stagnant pool, without
a brook to feed it. She'd carried a sense of
deep sadness for years without any idea of
where to search for spiritual freedom. Fubbi
Quantz had read its absence in her eyes.

But now, there was finally the light of
joy.

Great Freedom—Great Love

How do *you* pursue truth?

People will go to the far corners of the
world to find it. They'll go through one
religion after another; they'll become athe-
ists, maybe agnostics, and run through all
the different philosophies and religious
teachings.

But until they find love, they've not found truth.

And if they don't find love, they will never find freedom, spiritual freedom. So they are driven to search the world over looking for true love.

Is love so hard to find?

A Love Assignment

I write spiritual study courses for those who are students of the ECK teachings. In each monthly discourse, or letter, I try to pass along some spiritual insight as best I can.

But it's still up to people to put their creative faculties to work and get something out of each discourse.

A young mother who is an ECKist got one of these monthly discourses in the mail one day. In this particular discourse I asked people to do something purely for love without expecting anyone to say, "Thanks a lot for what you did; I appreciate it."

It was winter, and this woman likes to put out old bread and cereal for the birds and squirrels. The birds come from all around. But one particular day as she put out the bread, all that came were a squirrel and a crow.

She remembered that when she first started putting out food for the birds and the animals, she used to shoo away the crow and any other not-so-pretty birds. She thought that if she was going to put out food, it ought to be for the "pretty" birds.

But when she got this assignment in a monthly discourse—to do something just for love—she decided she would put out the food for any bird or animal that came. Of course, first in line are the squirrels and crows and sparrows.

It took a while, but soon she could accept all birds and all animals coming out to the feeding station in her yard. And with that change, love began to fill her heart.

How can you quantify love? It's not something you can take to the market and have people admire, or put up in an art gallery where people can say, "Oh, love! Look at that good example right there on the wall."

Love is just a very quiet, personal thing.

It brings fulfillment, but more importantly, it brings spiritual freedom. Because love is truth.

Freedom to Solve Our Problems

Soul is a spark of God. And we always have to say, too, that It is a creative spark of God.

When we have troubles and problems here on earth, it's easy to put out our hand like a little beggar boy and say, "Put something there because I want something." It's a form of creativity, begging, but it's not a very high form. There's an art to it, but it's not the best use of Soul's creativity.

There are other ways to draw upon the infinite abundance of life without having to grovel in the dirt like a beggar and act like a slave.

There are ways to recognize your God-hood, the Godness within you. To open yourself to help from Divine Spirit. To find out how to take care of yourself better.

Usually this means letting go of some of your old ideas of who and what you are.

Anton's Confrontation

When we discover Eckankar, the Path of Spiritual Freedom, we find life to be much richer than it was before. We also come to know some basic spiritual principles.

The first principle is this: Soul exists because God loves It. This means you exist because God loves you. Just knowing this gives a sense of freedom and joy to anyone who really knows what it means.

"Anton," an ECK student from Germany, used his divine creativity to help with a simple problem in his daily life.

One day he had to return something to a store. As he thought about the return, he felt that the salesman wasn't going to be open to taking back the item.

In his mind's eye, Anton could see the confrontation: the salesman would say, "I'm sorry, I can't take that back; you cannot return it." They would have words. And Anton might even leave the store with his purchase still on the counter as a sign of protest.

But instead of continuing in this direction, Anton made a decision. He said to himself, "I will leave my heart soft, like warm butter." Now, this is a bit of wisdom he had received in a dream: he found he could pass through walls in his dream experience if he kept his heart soft—soft like warm butter.

Anton had learned that as soon as he

became fearful, in a dream or in daily life, his heart turned cold. You know what happens to butter when it turns cold; it gets very firm like a brick.

So Anton went to the store and faced the clerk. He held this image in his mind's eye of melting butter, saying to himself, "My heart is like melting butter."

It worked. Anton returned his purchase.

A little help from divine creativity, and spiritual freedom from fear won the day. Maybe this is a technique that could work for you.

THE KEY TO LIBERATION

*T*he liberation of Soul comes in recognizing the Living ECK Master, who then leads us to the spiritual exercises which lead to the Sound and Light.

Then comes the liberation. This liberation is being freed from the endless cycle of birth and rebirth, from the pain and the sorrow and the unhappiness which come from being under the hand of fate, or destiny.

This is what we are looking for. Spiritual liberation comes at a point we call Self-Realization, which means that we have been freed from the cares of this world. I'm not saying that we no longer have problems, but we now have an understanding

27

of those things which come into our life that must be faced. We see where they came from, how we caused them, and what to do about them so that we can live a life of greater happiness.

Serena's Creative Potential

"Serena" had suffered chronic neck pain since childhood. So she asked the Mahanta, the Inner Master, for a healing and, by way of answer, had both a dream and a past-life recall.

In the dream a man she could not stand had proposed marriage. Since he did this before an audience of her high-school classmates, she felt obliged to spare him from embarrassment. Reluctantly, then, she accepted. But the ring he slipped on her finger had no precious stone in its setting. Later in the dream, she recalled speaking with a girlfriend about the unwelcome proposal. Serena confided how much she despised him. Yet she felt paralyzed, trapped.

So the next morning Serena tested her creative potential by doing a Spiritual Exercise of ECK.

During it she met the Mahanta, who revealed how he was helping her unwind a long-standing karmic pattern.

Serena had been a nurse and healer in past lives. It was in this manner that she'd developed a tendency of taking on the pain of others. Even so, what had begun as a natural expression of sympathy eventually became a burden and a scourge. Her pattern in this lifetime was to take on the grief and pain of others at the expense of her own well-being. What a karmic snare!

The dream was certainly showing that she'd wedded herself to a self-destructive practice.

She later read this article in the *Mystic World*, a quarterly publication for ECK members: "Why People Don't Find Spiritual Freedom." In it, she recognized a duty to create her own happiness. She did want to change old patterns. How could she reach the source of her problem?

For that reason Serena handed this karmic situation to the Mahanta and has since noticed a great weight come off her shoulders. She has finally recognized that the origin of her trying to please and care for the illnesses of others was but a mask for her own desire to get a spiritual healing. Now her service to others is healthy and more satisfying too. She gives for love and no longer from a mistaken sense of obligation.

For all that, Serena learned there was more to come.

A different day, in contemplation, the Inner Master brought to light Serena's past life as a religious figure in the early Christian era. She'd been a saintly woman, a nun. Her self-ordained mission was to convert prisoners, to try to save their souls before they were put to death. In this particular experience she saw herself in a long black habit. She marched resolutely on the heels of a prison guard who led the way to a murky dungeon and lit the dark passage with a smoky torch.

The pitiful wails of prisoners rose in the foul air. About to enter a cell armed only with her Bible, Serena dismissed the guard with an arrogant wave of her hand.

"Stand back," she said. "I walk with God."

She then entered the cell alone, ready to do God's bidding with some poor wretch of a sinner. Unfortunately that day's poor wretch of a sinner had decided to sin again. As a result he brutally clubbed the unsuspecting nun in the back of her head and neck with the chains that bound his wrists. The injuries were fatal.

Serena knew that this lifetime of pride in duty to save those she considered to be lesser Souls and the practice of taking on the emotional baggage of others were the reason for her chronic neck pain. She wanted to be rid of that burden from the past. So with the insights gained from her dream and contemplations, Serena could let go of her habit of taking on the emotional baggage of others. Moreover, she did physical exercises to strengthen her neck. Soon the pain was gone.

Serena thus learned a great secret: that her compulsion to save others was only an excuse to air her vanity. But she learned another fact. As her commitment to truth grows, the more she must give of God's love. Such was the great secret she'd learned from the Master.

Today Serena continues to walk with God, only now she does it much more wisely.

When we enter this world, we obtain certain abilities to carry us from cradle to grave. But if we choose to step on the spiritual path and make our way to God's kingdom, we have to earn a right to go there by learning other abilities.

So how do we do it?

We do it by learning to exercise our powers of imagination, to first visualize in great detail our world as we would have it. Everything around us today, from our choices in clothing to our placement with the family in which our rebirth occurred, is actually the outcome of attitudes we've formed over the centuries. We must form new attitudes if we wish to strike out in a new direction in our spiritual lives.

So how do we start?

We start to spiritualize our state of consciousness by learning the secrets of creative imagination. The doing of it comes through the Spiritual Exercises of ECK. In turn then, we see how upgrading our attitudes can bring into being a more pleasing and productive future for ourselves.

It can be a future alive with the blessing of spiritual freedom.

Purpose of the ECK Teachings

$\mathcal{E}$ach one of you is Soul, and it is your spiritual birthright to find the quickest route back to the highest states of spiritual being. This is what we are here to accomplish with the teachings of ECK.

What Have I to Give?

We find that the teachings of ECK are the teachings of the giver rather than of the receiver. Often when we begin on the path of ECK, we want to know, What can I gain for myself? Our initial motive is to gain in the way of love, spiritual unfoldment, material possessions, health, or in any number of other ways that concern us

34

in our everyday life.

But a natural change takes place as one begins to practice the Spiritual Exercises of ECK. These spiritual exercises are short periods of contemplation in which the individual who cares about the high, true aspects of life tries to make a connection with the spiritual life current.

Another name for this life current is the ECK, which is the Holy Spirit or the Holy Ghost spoken of in the Bible. But the definition of ECK goes beyond any description of the Holy Ghost or the Holy Spirit you have heard before. The ECK is the Word of God which is directly responsible for the creation of the worlds, including earth. God spoke, and the Word of God, the ECK, created all the worlds in all the universes of God.

These are lofty ideas which we generally don't run into in our daily life. Usually we are more concerned with how to make a living, take care of our family, and watch out for our health. Life today is so busy that sometimes we wonder if there is any truth or reality beyond our fast-paced daily existence.

Yet every moment of life offers the chance to give and receive divine love—the secret to spiritual freedom.

SECRETS OF MASTERSHIP

*P*eople who understand truth understand love and have love.

These people are self-responsible. They are strong in and of themselves. They go through the same hardships as other people, but they are the ones with an inner strength. Life will try to crush their spirit, but their strength comes not from any kind of material goods or a wealthy background. It is purely an inner strength.

They love unconditionally.

They love God because they know that God loves them. And anyone who truly knows this will find a great sense of freedom.

The Source of Freedom

On the inner planes* I was walking through the streets of a town in the manufacturing area. Two young boys came running after me; they were about ten or eleven. One called to me, "Can we come along with you?"

"Sure," I said.

We came to a huge warehouse, big enough to hold the Goodyear blimp. As soon as we went in, the boys began to jump around excitedly with a kind of joy. There was real freedom in this place.

"Do you know why you have this sense of freedom?" I asked them. They shook their heads; they didn't know. I said, "Look at the people in here."

For the first time, they looked around. The entire building was filled with crafts-

---

* The heavenly worlds contain many levels or planes. See the chart on page 41.

people, experts in their fields. There were master carpenters, master plumbers, computer operators, interior designers, artisans, and artists. They were remodeling the warehouse and creating things for people.

"Look at these people," I said again. "Each is an expert. They come here to do whatever they do better than anyone else. They get their satisfaction in life from doing a job well. Buyers come here expecting the finest, and they get it."

A young man in his midtwenties came walking by. He said, "I overheard you talking about what it takes to attain mastership and spiritual freedom," he said. "What did you do when you worked in a production phase like this?"

"I worked in printing," I said. "But whether it's printing or another craft, learning how to be careful and exact with what you do is the key. Do it for the love of God and not for the love of money."

I told the two young boys to come back again tomorrow, to watch the craftspeople at work. If the boys care enough about a task, some craftsperson might show them the secrets of how to become a master in that area.

These people were living spiritual freedom. And the first step to attaining this freedom is learning how to do something well because you love it, not because you're being paid to do it.

The lesson of the warehouse and the spirit of freedom that the young boys felt is this: Become an expert in something. You need to be grounded in something. When you do something for God, for the highest principle, you do each step until it sings.

Mastership is anything except just getting by.

THE WORLDS OF ECK

(Plane)	(Chant)	(Sound)
ANAMI LOK	HU *(HYOO)*	HU

AGAM LOK	HUK *(HOOK)*	MUSIC OF WOODWINDS
HUKIKAT LOK	ALUK *(ah-LOOK)*	THOUSAND VIOLINS
ALAYA LOK	HUM *(HYOOM)*	HUMMING SOUND
ALAKH LOK	SHANTI *(SHAHN-tee)*	WIND
ATMA LOK (Soul Plane)	SUGMAD *(SOOG-mahd)*	SINGLE NOTE OF A FLUTE

HIGHER WORLDS Positive   **GOD-REALIZATION**

ETHERIC (Intuition)   BAJU *(BAH-joo)*   BUZZING BEES

The last barrier between the lower worlds and the pure positive God Worlds.

- - - - - - - - - - - -

MENTAL (Mind)   AUM *(AHM or ah-UHM)*   RUNNING WATER

Source of all mental teachings, aesthetics, philosophies, conventional concepts of God, cosmic consciousness.

CAUSAL (Memory)   MANA *(MAH-nah)*   TINKLING BELLS

Plane where memories, karmic patterns, and Akashic records are stored. The Causal body is also the seed body. Plane of negative reality, which affects all below.

ASTRAL (Emotion)   KALA *(kah-LAH)*   ROAR OF THE SEA

Source of all psychic phenomena—ghosts, flying saucers, spirits, ESP. Plane reached by astral projection and most occult sciences.

PHYSICAL (Senses)   ALAYI *(ah-LAH-yee)*   THUNDER

Plane where Soul is trapped by the five passions: lust, anger, greed, vanity, and attachment. Plane of time, space, and matter. Illusion of reality.

LOWER WORLDS Negative   **SELF-REALIZATION**

You Came Here to Fly

$\mathcal{I}$ know an individual who once owned a hang glider. Whenever he got the urge, he would take it to a cliff, set it up, and go soaring off with the wind. He usually liked to go by himself, but one day he brought along a friend who had never flown a glider before. That day there was a strong wind blowing.

His friend was so anxious to give it a try that he ignored the instructions of the experienced hang-glider pilot. He took off running with the wing tipped too high. As soon as he got to the edge of the cliff, the wind caught the wing and blew him back.

The man who owned the glider repeated his instructions. "When you run into the wind, dip the wing down a little," he said. "Otherwise the glider could flip back on you." Then, almost as an afterthought, he added, "Remember, if you're going to fly, you don't want to go backward, you want to go forward."

His friend seemed to understand. Once again, he backed up and ran toward the cliff; but again, he neglected to keep the wing down. A strong gust of wind sent him somersaulting back across the field, and he and the glider went bouncing off into the distance.

The guy who owned the hang glider went running after him. When the glider stopped, his friend unhooked the safety harness. That wasn't very wise, because with no weight to secure it, the glider blew off with the wind.

The glider owner hesitated. He had a decision to make. Should he help his friend, or should he go after the hang glider? He looked back and forth, first at his friend, and then at the glider—blowing farther and farther away.

Finally he decided his friend would still be there; he was too dazed to walk. He ran after his hang glider, secured it to himself, and brought it back to where the other man was waiting.

His friend was just sitting there shaking his head. "That thing is really dangerous," he said. "You shouldn't go hang gliding by yourself. Look what happened to me. If you had been up here alone, you might have gotten hurt, and there wouldn't have been anyone around to help you."

The fellow with the glider just looked at his friend for a moment. He was trying to find a way to explain to him that he had failed because he wouldn't pay attention to how it should be done. Finally he said, "Look, I came here to fly, not to fall."

His outlook on life was to focus on the

moment. First he took the time to learn how to operate the glider correctly and to study the rules of safety. Then he went forward with confidence, never worrying about what might happen if the wind bounced him back.

The Spiritual Survivor

If you came here to fly, then fly. But if your fears are holding you back, unconsciously you will tip the wing too high in the wind, go bouncing back, and end up in a tangled wreckage. It takes courage to do what you started out to do.

If you came here to fly, you must take responsibility for your own spiritual life. First know where you are going, and then do what it takes to get there. Look for the open doors, and know there is always a way out.

Wherever you go, expect the most from life, and be willing to pay the price. When you can do this, you will have become the spiritual survivor who will survive under any conditions; and when you have finished your experiences on earth, you will have gained an incredible degree of strength and courage. You will be prepared to face the worlds to come with confidence, knowing you are protected by the hand of the Holy Spirit.

Take your share of drubbings, because within each lesson is hidden the seed of truth which is needed for you to take the step that follows. But you can't take the next step until you take the step that is right here. You must begin where you are now.

If you ask God to show you truth, but you haven't used your talents today, then you can't expect to find the greater talents and the greater truth tomorrow. The way is always through the Spiritual Exercises of ECK.

You Can Go Beyond

*W*e always go back to the Spiritual Exercises of ECK, because these lead to Self-Realization and God-Realization, and from this come the attributes of wisdom, charity, and freedom.

If you are willing to do so, you can go beyond your present state of consciousness by examining yourself honestly, not with the mind but with the faculties of Soul.

These faculties are awakened and enlivened through the Spiritual Exercises of ECK, in which one listens for the Sound of God or looks for the Light of God through chanting *HU*, which is a love song to God. There are also a number of other sounds that can be used to uplift the individual spiritually.

Several of these words are listed on the chart on page 41.

Your Passkey to Life

The Spiritual Exercises of ECK are the lost passkey to life. They give the secrets of the ancient ones. Why be life's victim? A greater state of consciousness is a direct result of doing your spiritual exercises and will reveal new ways to ease your life.

Such freedom is but one of the many benefits that come to all who wish to find the living way and do something about it.

The Miraculous Power of Your Imagination

Soul is a reflection of the ECK, for It was created from this Spirit and given free will to make choices.

Soul's attributes include both intelligence and imagination, and hence It can postulate and create things. It is the spark of eternal being that God has tucked within human and other material forms to animate them. As a result, Soul is like God in that It enjoys an inventive nature that sees no limitations.

The creative imagination is God's special gift to us, which develops along two lines: the mental and spiritual. The spiritual line creates things of a higher and finer nature than anything the mind could ever conceive of. The mind, on the other hand, is at its finest when it is like a surgical tool for the projects of Soul.

The creative imagination is vital in that it gives people a way to help bring the greatest spiritual blessings into their lives. So what begins as imagination ends as a doorway to heaven. Yet it can influence the workings in this world too.

Training the Imagination

The imaginative faculty within yourself is like a muscle; you're going to have to train it day after day. Experiment. Set up enjoyable things to do on the inner planes. If one technique doesn't work for you, then modify it, adapt it, experiment. Do whatever you can.

The Mahanta, the Living ECK Master tries to find ways to help people who are on the borderline of orthodox thought and seeking the real truth. He tries to help them explore the inner worlds so they can gain more wisdom and freedom. This is part of spiritual liberation. It is part of the package of God Consciousness—to be fully, universally aware of your own worlds at all hours of the day and night.

The purpose of the Living ECK Master is to help each Soul find liberation from the wheel of reincarnation. It is not necessary to wait until after death to attain freedom.

An invitation is extended to any true seeker who wants to find for himself the Light and Sound of God. This treasure is

the birthright of Soul that leads to the kingdom of heaven.

SPIRITUAL EXERCISES: TRY OUT YOUR WINGS

To get around barriers on the road to God, an individual must find the Sound and Light, the most certain way to spiritual freedom.

A simple contemplative exercise to help you do that is this: At bedtime, shut your eyes and look at a blank screen in your mind. This screen is located at the Spiritual Eye, which is slightly above and behind the eyebrows. Breathe deeply several times, then sing *God* or *HU* softly for ten to twenty minutes.

Before contemplation, think of some person you love, or of some happy event.

This feeling of love or goodwill will help open your heart to God.

You may experience a feeling of peace, warmth in your heart, or a wave of gratitude. Enjoy this sacred time at the temple within yourself.

A Spiritual Exercise on the Mountain of God

This is a technique of the imagination.

Find a quiet place for this spiritual exercise where no one will disturb you for ten or fifteen minutes. Then shut your eyes and look behind and between your eyebrows. That is the location of your Spiritual Eye.

Now imagine you are climbing to the top of a broad green mountain. Follow the dirt path that leads to a meadow dressed in a carpet of bright, cheerful flowers. Powder-white clouds kiss the summit of the mountain and will instill in you a sense of great joy and wonder.

That is the Mountain of God.

When you reach the top, lie upon the thick, soft carpet of luxurious grass. Feel the sunshine play on your face, arms, and body. Now shut your eyes there on the mountain, too, as you did at the beginning of this spiritual exercise.

Then look gently but steadily into your Spiritual Eye for the Light of God. While waiting for It to appear, sing *HU* slowly, again and again.

The Light may appear as a soft field of light, similar to the soft white clouds above the mountain. Or it may be a pinpoint of light—blue, white, yellow, purple, or even green or pink.

Continue to watch for the Light within your Spiritual Eye. Now also start listening for the Sound of God—the vibration of the Holy Spirit moving the atoms of life. You may hear It as the sound of a flute, a rushing wind, the chirping of birds, a crashing waterfall, ringing bells, or the buzzing of bees. These are actual, not imaginary, sounds.

This dual manifestation of the Voice of God can bring you more love, wisdom, and understanding.

Let the experience be all you can imagine it to be—and maybe even more.

QUESTIONS AND ANSWERS

*A*s spiritual leader of Eckankar, I get thousands of letters from seekers of truth around the world. All want direct and useful answers about how to travel the road to God. Here are several questions I've been asked relating to spiritual freedom.

Spiritual Freedom for Others

How do I balance what I want and still leave other people their freedom? Especially when my desires involve others?

Let's say a person wanted companionship. He might put the request to Divine Spirit, then do those things out here that he had to do to get ready—shave, dress nicely, whatever. Then he would leave the results to Spirit.

But if the person directs his request, saying, "That is the person I would like to share my life with," maybe his desire is not part of that other person's life scheme. He'll probably find that what he imagines won't come true. It gets into the freedom of another individual.

When you don't put a definite shape to what you imagine, Divine Spirit can have unlimited freedom to fill that mold. But if you put a limit to it, you often strike out because you've allowed for only one possible outcome.

Career Choice Freedom

I am trying to decide about a future career. I was wondering how important a college education is today. Also, does God care what one does in regard to a career, or is that up to the individual Soul? Is there some way I can tap into what God wants me to do?

How important is college today? It depends upon where you live and your cultural background. Pockets of golden opportunities dot the earth. Everything is of the ECK (Holy Spirit). We live where we do because of what there is to learn there.

Allow yourself a lot of breathing room when picking a career. If you lock on to a certain profession too soon, you will miss many chances to grow spiritually. Yet in the meantime learn all you can, no matter where you live. Learn for the joy of it. If your goal is purely to get rich, you will box yourself into a dull life.

Times and conditions change for each generation. A secret I've found that always helped for promotion was to do as well as I could in everything. Success has a way of finding those who always do their best.

God just wants you to become a Co-worker. You can be that anytime and in any place.

First Step in Loving God

From a religious point of view, what is the importance of a physical relationship while obtaining spiritual freedom?

A loving relationship is the first step to loving God. Love unties the bonds that anchor us to the material world of wants and desires. So divine love leads directly to spiritual freedom.

The steps to spiritual freedom are these: (1) learn to love yourself, (2) learn to love others (human love), and (3) this will open your heart to love for God. That is the key to spiritual freedom.

Your journey to God begins at home.

Soul's Goal

What is the ultimate goal of Soul?

Here is a brief review of the final goal of Soul: It gathers an education in the lower worlds so that It can become a true citizen in the spiritual community. This is what we call a Co-worker with God.

The relationship between parent and child in the worlds of matter is based on this spiritual design. The parent is the vehicle for the child's entrance into the world and is responsible for his education. The child must, between birth and the age of perhaps eighteen, learn all the dos and don'ts of his culture. The significant fact underlying the parent-child relationship is that there is more freedom for the child as he gets older and assumes more responsibility. The parent has failed his duties if the child reaches legal age and is unfit to take his place in the world.

The path of Eckankar encourages the freedom and responsibility of Soul. After all, that is Its birthright.

Every Soul is a spark of God. The child learns by making errors, but the wise parent must let the child learn for himself, giving guidance when it is necessary.

Your Key to Freedom

A crisis at work brought up a question. I thought I did not care about death; if my time came, I felt I was ready. But now I realize I do have that fear, and during the recent incident at work, I could not face it in someone else.

ECK is an active path. We recognize that each experience that comes our way is spiritually instructive. If someone needs our help, we do what we can to the best of our ability.

A crisis such as you faced may be the Mahanta's way to kindle a new respect in you for the opportunity of this life. At the same time, the experience makes one dip into the well of reflection, to broaden compassion for an individual in trouble.

As you realized, fear of death has hidden itself in you. Now think about it: if there's room for fear of death, there is also room for its counterpart—a fear of living. On the path of ECK you will find that fear will diminish its hold on your life. There is the beginning of love.

Keep up with the Spiritual Exercises of ECK. They're your key to freedom.

Growing in Consciousness

Why don't troubles go away once we ask for help?

Much of the trouble we have in life is a result of some long-standing negative attitude. It has created these situations. Soul, the spiritual being you are, gains experience as It works through these rough spots on the road.

Some of our troubles will be dispelled by Divine Spirit while others are not. They are part of the divine plan for Soul to gain the purification or change in consciousness so It can know what It is.

It needs to know why It has reincarnated into today's family and business environment.

Many people do not understand that life, with its burdens, is a treasure. The weight of disappointment makes us close our eyes to the gift of being in the world to learn about the loving heart.

Soul's Freedom

In a dream I walked up into some hills, and it seemed like the Fourth of July. Thousands of people were sitting on the hillsides looking into the sky as if expecting fireworks. The sky was light blue and free of clouds.

I walked past the crowds until I was alone again and looked at the hills in the distance. They were like hard-packed sand dunes without vegetation. Suddenly, a flash of red went by and stopped long enough for me to recognize it before disappearing. It was me. That made me feel really odd. Looking out over the ridge of hills, I saw they had undergone a drastic change. They were much lumpier, and a huge boulder with green vines all over it had been raised ten feet into the air.

The dream felt very real. I had just gone through a doorway and was expecting a member of an ancient American race that I had just read about in a Louis L'Amour novel. But I woke up before he arrived.

This is what your dream means: Your walk up into the hills indicates that in the dream you were moving into a higher state of consciousness.

The Fourth of July is Independence Day for Americans. This image evokes the ideal of spiritual freedom, which you can achieve in this lifetime if you set your heart upon it.

The thousands of people are your collective awareness—i.e., the sum total of your thoughts and hopes. You are awaiting the ecstasy of spiritual freedom. When you leave the crowds, it means you leave behind your worries and come to rest in Soul, the center of your being.

You are now in the Soul body and look

64

back on the hills, which are nothing more than events in your daily life. From the lofty vantage point of Soul, your outer life seems to be a spiritual wasteland, especially when you let anger (the "flash of red") flare up.

The image of the boulder is used in a double sense here. First, Soul studies the ridge of hills to see what harm anger might do, and It perceives a "much lumpier" life. Anger makes mountains out of molehills, or in this case, a huge boulder is raised ten feet into the air.

Second, green vines clinging to the face of the boulder show the power of envy or jealousy to undermine a relationship. Have you heard the phrase "green with envy"? The roots of the vines can, in time, shatter the greatest boulder, just as envy and jealousy can destroy the closest relationship, even one that seems "solid as a rock."

The member of an ancient American race whom you were expecting was the

Mahanta, the Living ECK Master.

This dream gives a most exacting look at yourself to help you better understand yourself.

Times of Need

I've recently been informed that I will soon be out of a job. My career and future job possibilities here are ruined. I would be grateful to know what brought all this on.

The moment you drop your letter of request in the mailbox, the ECK begins to work to bring the spiritual upliftment that you need in times of trouble. Its first concern is that you have the purification needed to take you into the high spiritual planes.

Crises and troubles push us against the small self within us. The conflict between what we think our life should be and what the ECK has in store for us is quickly resolved in favor of the individual's spiritual growth.

The greater spiritual advances are made in times of extreme stress. When there's no place else to go, true surrender of our cares and worries to the Mahanta occurs. The Holy Spirit provides a way out of the darkest, most threatening circumstances.

Standing Up

How can I be a spiritual student and still stand up for what I believe in, such as the abortion issue?

The abortion issue is an emotional one. If you believe in something, do what you can through community groups already established. This is how the spiritual student becomes a vehicle in a quiet way, standing behind issues that he feels strongly about, issues that threaten to rob him of basic freedoms of choice.

Then if you can find other ways to blend in a spiritual viewpoint, this gives added impetus. Let people do what is comfortable for them, because that is where their talents will shine. The fight to preserve our freedoms is unending and will change faces again and again. The ultimate purpose of the negative power is to enslave Soul in the clutches of the materialistic world. It is that simple.

These are perhaps the most trying, yet most significant times ever encountered by people in their search for truth. In truth, the path of the Master is his own path. Although we can learn from his experiences, our unfoldment depends entirely upon our own encounters with the nitty-gritty of life.

Adjusting to a New Life

About four years ago I moved from my hometown to a foreign country. Newly wed, my heart full of love, I thought all obstacles would be leveled by time and love. I was wrong. I still cannot adapt to this new country and language, and I feel lonely. I need to find peace of mind and get rid of this feeling of being a bird without wings.

Often the Holy Spirit has reasons for

putting us where we are until we've learned certain spiritual lessons. It is true that most of us feel more comfortable around our friends and loved ones. In a way, you are homesick. This experience is making you very much aware that you, as Soul, are also separated from your true spiritual home.

In you is awakened the desire to return to God. This spiritual side has a physical counterpart: your desire to someday return to your country. If that is the only way you feel you can ever be happy again, let Divine Spirit work out this problem for you. It may take time, for Spirit works in Its own way and in Its own time to bring relief to those who ask.

A way to let the ECK, or Holy Spirit, guide your life is to say inwardly (and often), "Thy will be done."

Freedom from Suffering

I've let my fears really mess me up. Should my goal always be to choose my own way of

life no matter what others think of my deci-
sions? Deep down, I know this is true, and yet
it's hard to break loose of a feeling that insists
I must suffer in this life.

In general, let me say that people will intrude upon our good nature for their own negative purposes if we let them.

It is simply a matter of catching them at their game, then slowly but gradually, over a period of time, letting ourselves be less accessible to them.

It is part of the freedom we can develop for ourselves by adopting a different attitude about what others will think. With practice, we get better at handling the subtle pressures and guilts that are thrown at us, especially if someone is attempting to bend our will to fit their own.

Often, it is enough to sing *HU*, the ancient name of God, inwardly and silently whenever in the presence of a person who is intruding into our psychic space. Singing

HU either opens us to direct help from Divine Spirit or else gives us the insight on how to handle the next step in this situation ourselves.

I want you to know that the love and protection of the ECK, the Holy Spirit, is always with you.

WHICH WAY NOW?

$\mathcal{Y}$our experiences here on earth offer a chance to develop the beauty and grace necessary for a Co-worker with God.

When the season is right, each of us finds the ancient, yet ever-new, teachings of ECK and can now set out on the most ecstatic adventure of a lifetime, the journey to God.

All of us must make dozens and dozens of which-way-now? decisions at important crossroads during the course of our many lifetimes. But at the end of the road is the Mahanta, who receives all with great joy. And we're never again alone from that moment on.

The route to light and truth is quicker

for some than others. All depends upon Soul's determination.

What is life other than us meeting ourselves in the play of the world?

The odyssey of Soul teaches us to cooperate with the laws of God. When we've learned to do that, the highest, purest, and finest love in all the far-flung worlds of God is ours.

You may be sure that this spiritual odyssey is worth every single moment.

NEXT STEPS IN
SPIRITUAL EXPLORATION

- **Try a spiritual exercise.**
  Review the spiritual exercises in this book or
  on our website.
  Experiment with them.

- **Browse our website: www.Eckankar.org.**
  Watch videos; get free books, answers to
  FAQs, and more info.

- **Attend a spiritual event in your area.**
  Visit "Eckankar around the World" on
  our website.

- **Begin your journey** with the Eckankar spiritual self-discovery courses that come with
  membership.

- **Read additional books** about the ECK
  teachings.

- **Call or write to us:** Call 1-800-LOVE GOD
  (1-800-568-3463, toll-free, automated) or
  (952) 380-2200 (direct).

- Write to: ECKANKAR, Dept. BK130, PO Box
  2000, Chanhassen, MN 55317-2000 USA.

FOR FURTHER READING
By Harold Klemp

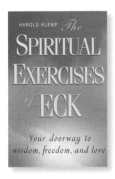

The Spiritual Exercises of ECK

This book is a staircase with 131 steps leading to the doorway to spiritual freedom, self-mastery, wisdom, and love. A comprehensive volume of spiritual exercises for every need.

ECK Wisdom on Conquering Fear

Would having more courage and confidence help you make the most of this lifetime?

Going far beyond typical self-help advice, this book invites you to explore divine love as the antidote to anxiety and the doorway to inner freedom.

You will discover ways to identify the karmic roots

of fear and align with your highest ideals.

Use this book to soar beyond your limitations and reap the benefits of self-mastery.

Live life to its fullest potential!

ECK Wisdom on Dreams

This dream study will help you be more *awake* than you've ever been!

ECK Wisdom on Dreams reveals the most ancient of dream teachings for a richer and more productive life today.

In this dynamic book, author Harold Klemp shows you how to remember your dreams, apply dream wisdom to everyday situations, recognize prophetic dreams, and more.

You will be introduced to the art of dream interpretation and offered techniques to discover the treasures of your inner worlds.

ECK Wisdom on Inner Guidance

Looking for answers, guidance, protection?

Help can come as a nudge, a dream, a vision, or a quiet voice within you. This book offers new ways to connect with the ever-present guidance of ECK, the Holy Spirit. Start today!

Discover how to listen to the Voice of God; attune to your true self; work with an inner guide; benefit from dreams, waking dreams, and Golden-tongued Wisdom; and ignite your creativity to solve problems.

Each story, technique, and spiritual exercise is a doorway to greater confidence and love for life.

Open your heart, and let God's voice speak to you!

ECK Wisdom on Karma and Reincarnation

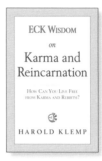

Have you lived before? What is the real meaning of life?

Discover your divine destiny—to move beyond the limits of karma and reincarnation and gain spiritual freedom.

This book reveals the purpose of living and the keys to spiritual growth.

You'll find answers to age-old questions about fate, destiny, and free will. These gems of wisdom can enhance your relationships, health, and happiness—and offer the chance to resolve all your karma in this lifetime!

ECK Wisdom on Life after Death

All that lies ahead is already within your heart.

ECK Wisdom on Life after Death invites you to explore the eternal nature of you!

Author Harold Klemp offers you new perspectives on seeing heaven before you die, meeting with departed loved ones, near-death experiences, getting help from spiritual guides, animals in heaven, and dealing with grief.

Try the techniques and spiritual exercise included in this book to find answers and explore the secrets of life after death—-for yourself.

ECK Wisdom on Solving Problems

Problems? Problems! Why do we have so many? What causes them? Can we avoid them?

Author Harold Klemp, the spiritual leader of Eckankar, can help you answer these questions and more. His sense of humor and practical approach offer spiritual keys to unlock the

secrets to effective problem solving. Learn creative, time-tested techniques to

- Find the root cause of a problem
- Change your viewpoint and overcome difficulties
- Conquer your fears
- Work beyond symptoms to solutions
- Kindle your creativity

79

- Master your karma, past and present
- Receive spiritual guidance that can transform the way you see yourself and your life

Spiritual Wisdom on Health and Healing

This booklet is rich with spiritual keys to better health on every level.

Discover the spiritual roots of illness and how gratitude can open your heart to God's love and healing.

Simple spiritual exercises go deep to help you get personal divine guidance and insights.

Revitalize your connection with the true healing power of God's love.

Spiritual Wisdom on Prayer, Meditation, and Contemplation

Bring balance and wonder to your life!

This booklet is a portal to your direct, personal connection with Divine Spirit.

Harold Klemp shows how you can experience the powerful benefits of contemplation—"a conversation with the most secret, most genuine, and most mysterious part of yourself."

Move beyond traditional meditation via dynamic spiritual exercises. Learn about the uplifting chant of HU (an ancient holy name for God), visualization, creative imagination, and other active techniques.

Spiritual Wisdom on Relationships

Find the answers to common questions of the heart, including the truth about soul mates, how to strengthen a marriage, and how to know if a partnership is worth developing.

The spiritual exercises included in this booklet can help you break a pattern of poor relationships and find balance. You'll learn new ways to open your heart to love and enrich your relationship with God.

This booklet is a key for anyone wanting more love to give, more love to get. It's a key to better relationships with everyone in your life.

The Call of Soul

Discover how to find spiritual freedom in this lifetime and the infinite world of God's love for you. Includes a CD with dream and Soul Travel techniques.

HU, the Most Beautiful Prayer

Singing *HU*, the ancient name for God, can open your heart and lead you to a new understanding of yourself. Includes a CD of the HU song.

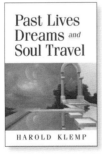

Past Lives, Dreams, and Soul Travel

These stories and exercises help you find your true purpose, discover greater love than you've ever known, and learn that spiritual freedom is within reach.

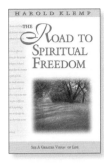

The Road to Spiritual Freedom, Mahanta Transcripts, Book 17

Sri Harold's wisdom and heart-opening stories of everyday people having extraordinary experiences tell of a secret truth at work in *your* life—there is divine purpose and meaning to every experience you have.

How to Survive Spiritually in Our Times, Mahanta Transcripts, Book 16

Discover how to reinvent yourself spiritually—to thrive in a changing world. Stories, tools, techniques, and spiritual insights to apply in your life now.

Autobiography of a Modern Prophet

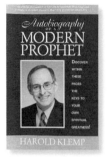

This riveting story of Harold Klemp's climb up the Mountain of God will help you discover the keys to your own spiritual greatness.

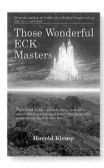

Those Wonderful ECK Masters

Would you like to have *personal* experience with spiritual masters that people all over the world—since the beginning of time—have looked to for guidance, protection, and divine love? This book includes real-life stories and spiritual exercises to meet eleven ECK Masters.

The Spiritual Laws of Life

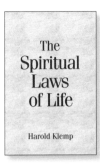

Learn how to keep in tune with your true spiritual nature. Spiritual laws reveal the behind-the-scenes forces at work in your daily life.

Available at bookstores, from online booksellers, or directly from Eckankar: www.ECKBooks.org; (952) 380-2222; ECKANKAR, Dept. BK130, PO Box 2000, Chanhassen, MN 55317-2000 USA.

Glossary

Words set in SMALL CAPS are defined elsewhere in this glossary.

Blue Light   How the MAHANTA often appears in the inner worlds to the CHELA or seeker.

chela   A spiritual student. Often a member of ECKANKAR.

ECK   The Life Force, the Holy Spirit, or Audible Life Current which sustains all life.

Eckankar *EHK-ahn-kahr*   The Path of Spiritual Freedom. Also known as the Ancient Science of SOUL TRAVEL. A truly spiritual way of life for the individual in modern times. The teachings provide a framework for anyone to explore their own spiritual experiences. Established by PAUL TWITCHELL, the modern-day founder, in 1965. The word means Co-worker with God.

ECK Masters   Spiritual Masters who can assist and protect people in their spiritual studies and travels. The ECK Masters are from a long line of God-Realized SOULS who know the responsibility that goes with spiritual freedom.

Fubbi Quantz The guardian of the Shariyat-Ki-Sugmad at the Katsupari Monastery in northern Tibet. He was the Mahanta, the Living ECK Master during the time of Buddha, about 500 BC.

God-Realization The state of God Consciousness. Complete and conscious awareness of God.

HU *HYOO* The most ancient, secret name for God. It can be sung as a love song to God aloud or silently to oneself to align with God's love.

Karma, Law of The Law of Cause and Effect, action and reaction, justice, retribution, and reward, which applies to the lower or psychic worlds: the Physical, Astral, Causal, Mental, and Etheric Planes.

Klemp, Harold The present Mahanta, the Living ECK Master. Sri Harold Klemp became the Mahanta, the Living ECK Master in 1981. His spiritual name is Wah Z.

Living ECK Master The spiritual leader of Eckankar. He leads Soul back to God. He teaches in the physical world as the Outer Master, in the dream state as the Dream Master, and in the spiritual worlds as the Inner Master. Sri Harold Klemp became the Mahanta, the Living ECK Master in 1981.

Mahanta An expression of the Spirit of God that is always with you. Sometimes seen as a Blue Light or Blue Star or in the form of the

Mahanta, the Living ECK Master. The highest state of God Consciousness on earth, only embodied in the Living ECK Master. He is the Living Word.

planes Levels of existence, such as the Physical, Astral, Causal, Mental, Etheric, and Soul Planes.

Self-Realization Soul recognition. The entering of Soul into the Soul Plane and there beholding Itself as pure Spirit. A state of seeing, knowing, and being.

Shariyat-Ki-Sugmad The sacred scriptures of Eckankar. The scriptures are comprised of twelve volumes in the spiritual worlds. The first two were transcribed from the inner planes by Paul Twitchell, modern-day founder of Eckankar.

Soul The True Self, an individual, eternal spark of God. The inner, most sacred part of each person. Soul can see, know, and perceive all things. It is the creative center of Its own world.

Soul Travel The expansion of consciousness. The ability of Soul to transcend the physical body and travel into the spiritual worlds of God. Soul Travel is taught only by the Living ECK Master. It helps people unfold spiritually and can provide proof of the existence of God and life after death.

Sound and Light of ECK   The Holy Spirit. The two aspects through which God appears in the lower worlds. People can experience them by looking and listening within themselves and through Soul Travel.

Spiritual Exercises of ECK   Daily practices for direct, personal experiences with the Sound Current. Creative techniques using contemplation and the singing of sacred words to bring the higher awareness of Soul into daily life.

Sri   *SREE*   A title of spiritual respect, similar to reverend or pastor, used for those who have attained the Kingdom of God. In Eckankar, it is reserved for the Mahanta, the Living ECK Master.

Sugmad   *SOOG-mahd*   A sacred name for God. It is the source of all life, neither male nor female, the Ocean of Love and Mercy.

Temples of Golden Wisdom   Golden Wisdom Temples found on the various planes—from the Physical to the Anami Lok; chelas of Eckankar are taken to these temples in the Soul body to be educated in the divine knowledge; sections of the Shariyat-Ki-Sugmad, the sacred teachings of ECK, are kept at these temples.

Twitchell, Paul   An American ECK Master who brought the modern teachings of Eckankar to the world through his writings and lectures. His spiritual name is Peddar Zaskq.

Wah Z *WAH zee* The spiritual name of SRI HAROLD KLEMP. It means the secret doctrine. It is his name in the spiritual worlds.

For more explanations of ECKANKAR terms, see *A Cosmic Sea of Words: The ECKANKAR Lexicon*, by Harold Klemp.

ABOUT THE AUTHOR

Award-winning author, teacher, and spiritual guide Sri Harold Klemp helps seekers reach their full potential.

He is the Mahanta, the Living ECK Master and spiritual leader of Eckankar, the Path of Spiritual Freedom. He is the latest in a long line of spiritual Adepts who have served throughout history in every culture of the world.

Sri Harold teaches creative spiritual practices that enable anyone to achieve life mastery and gain inner peace and contentment. His messages are relevant to today's spiritual needs and resonate with every generation.

Sri Harold's body of work includes more than one hundred books, which have been translated into eighteen languages and won multiple awards. The miraculous, true-life stories he shares lift the veil between heaven and earth.

In his groundbreaking memoir, *Autobiography of a Modern Prophet*, he reveals secrets to spiritual success gleaned from his personal journey into the heart of God.

Find your own path to true happiness, wisdom, and love in Sri Harold Klemp's inspired writings.